The Library of
E-Commerce and Internet Careers

E-Commerce
Careers
in
Multimedia

Carla Romaine Cowan

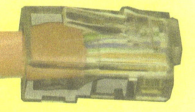

The Rosen Publishing Group, Inc.
New York

Published in 2001 by The Rosen Publishing Group, Inc.
29 East 21st Street, New York, NY 10010

Library of Congress Cataloging-in-Publication Data

Cowan, Carla Romaine.
E-Commerce careers in multimedia / Carla Romaine Cowan. —
1st ed.
p. cm. — (The library of e-commerce and internet careers)
Includes bibliographical references and index.
ISBN: 978-1-4358-8759-6
1. Multimedia systems—Vocational guidance—Juvenile litera-
ture. [1. Multimedia systems—Vocational guidance. 2. Vocational
guidance.] I. Title. II. Series.
QA76.575 .C685 2001
006.7'023'73--dc21

2001001498

Manufactured in the United States of America

Table of Contents

Introduction ——————————— 4

1 What Is Multimedia? ——————— 7

2 Multimedia Basics ——————— 20

3 Anatomy of a Multimedia Project ——— 30

4 Careers in Multimedia ——————— 41

5 Getting Started ——————— 47

Glossary ———————————— 53

For More Information ——————— 59

For Further Reading ——————— 61

Index ————————————— 62

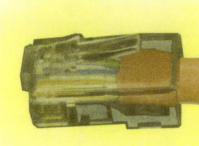

Introduction

Careers in the multimedia industry cover a broad range of activities. They can include projects such as the creation of a static Web page created by anyone with access to the Internet, to a complex, interactive game that reacts to a player's actions. Multimedia can be defined as anything that combines text, sound, graphics, video, and interactivity.

The birth of multimedia can be traced from the late 1970s, when Apple Computer revolutionized the way that computers displayed information. Shortly after, the ability to create presentations containing a combination of text and graphics formed the basis for multimedia applications. Sue Ann Ambron coined the word "multimedia" when she founded Apple Computer's first multimedia lab.

The introduction of the CD-ROM in the 1980s was a major step for multimedia because interactivity was introduced. Interactivity allowed people to become engaged with the computer. With the invention of the CD-ROM, complex programs with text, graphics, audio, video, and interactivity became popular and accessible to many computer users. The CD-ROM was the newest way to present any information that needed to be dynamic and engaging, from educational resources to product presentations.

The fast-growing popularity of the Internet has pushed the multimedia industry into a new stage of life. Businesses must now compete to gain attention, and plain text and unimaginative imagery will no longer do the trick. The Internet generation demands rich media experiences that grab its attention while shopping, surfing, or even researching.

Multimedia careers are fast-paced, creative, and exciting. A diverse set of people is needed for the creation of any multimedia project, including content creators such as writers and artists, animators, software developers, graphic designers, audio and video producers, and project producers.

The combination of e-commerce and multimedia experiences used to be seen as a technical disadvantage for e-tailers, or retail stores that have put up Web sites to sell goods. Customers with slow Internet connections were missing out on many of the detailed

From any site in the Gap network, Web users can access Gap, Inc. to see new products, find career opportunities, and even apply for jobs.

graphics and animations. These graphics were far too complex to stream quickly, causing viewers to move to other, faster Web sites. However, today's most popular retailers all use some form of multimedia. Whether in the form of in-store kiosks (public computer stations set up by retailers to allow customers to gain more access to product information or company Web sites) or animated ad banners and company logos used by e-tailers on the Web, multimedia is here to stay. It is one of the newest, most dynamic, and most popular industries.

What Is Multimedia?

The term "multimedia" simply means a combination of more than one type of media. Media refers to any type of content that can be presented in a digital format—including text, graphics, audio, and video. Industry professionals refer to multimedia as rich media.

Multimedia, or rich media, is the combination of several types of media (text, graphics, audio, and video) to create a compelling display of information. From simple presentations to complex virtual-reality games, the multimedia industry transforms dull and static content into rich, memorable experiences.

Multimedia is used in a wide variety of ways to supplement the efforts of similar industries. Animated Web advertising banners, Web design that incorporates interactivity and animation, educational tools that simulate live experiences, gaming Web sites, CD-ROMs, and Web-based television and radio stations are all examples of multimedia.

TRANSFORMING STATIC CONTENT INTO RICH MEDIA

All multimedia projects begin with an idea and perhaps some existing content. Usually, this content is referred to as static content because it does not change on its own. Static content normally includes text and simple graphics only.

Multimedia applications may be very simple, such as creating an animated graphic or adding a sound or video clip to an existing Web site. A more complex multimedia application would involve creating animations that respond to something the user does, such as clicking on a "button" or "hot spot" to start sound. Another multimedia application could have video appear in response to the user's selecting an item from a drop-down menu. The more complex a multimedia application is, the more skills a designer must have to create the final product.

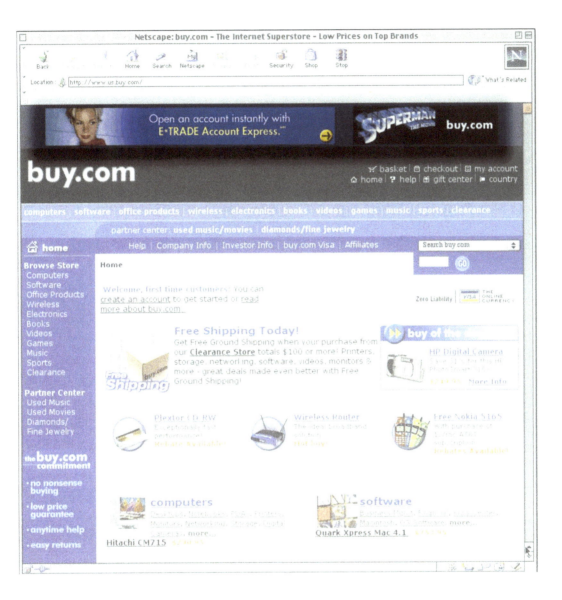

Banner ads such as the ones shown on Buy.com's Web site enable Web users to directly access another company's site from the one they are visiting.

Combining images from different sources creates multimedia content. These images can be from a variety of sources, such as still or digital photographs, illustrations, or other digital images. Each image may be manipulated (changed) using software programs such as Flash, Director, or simple GIF animation programs. More information on these programs will be provided in chapter 2. Audio and video must be converted to a digital format or initially designed using equipment that creates digital formats.

Planning is the key to successfully transforming static content to rich media. To use rich media effectively, it must be put together to form a compelling experience for the user. A Web site with sound clips, video clips, and moving images that operate separately will be confusing rather than entertaining or informative. In contrast, a Web site that uses audio and video with text and images to convey a single message will be much more engaging for its users.

MULTIMEDIA AND E-COMMERCE

Although the multimedia industry is responsible for creating many exciting applications, the use of multimedia goes far beyond gaming. Multimedia is used in very practical ways to assist customers every day. Put simply, e-commerce is buying and selling goods on the Web. There are many different types of e-commerce, but the term usually indicates one of two types: business to consumer (B2C) or business to business (B2B). B2C e-commerce happens anytime a person buys an item from an e-tailer, whereas B2B e-commerce occurs when businesses buy and sell from one another over the Web. E-commerce is so popular because the act of exchanging information electronically changes the entire scope of traditional business activities. E-commerce eliminates geographic barriers, offers customers and businesses greater flexibility, and creates new jobs that were never available before. To demonstrate just how important e-commerce is going to be in the future, statisticians predict that worldwide sales from online businesses will be close to $3.2 trillion dollars by 2003. Some examples of e-commerce multimedia include the following e-tailers.

CDNOW

The popular e-tailer CDNOW creates a richer experience for its users by adding multimedia to its Web site. Users can listen to sound samples of music in multiple formats and can watch video clips of movies. This rich media experience helps CDNOW give its shoppers a demonstration of the products it sells. Many times, because shoppers are given an opportunity to sample

A Sampling of the Multimedia World

This chart outlines the varying complexities of multimedia projects, the types of media used to produce them, and the possible job titles of the people involved.

Project Type	Media Used	Talent Needed
A static Web site with video or sound clips	Text Images Audio or video already formatted	Producer Writer Graphic designer Web developer
A static Web site with noninteractive animation	Text Images Simple animation files	Producer Writer Graphic designer Animator Web developer
A CD-ROM with sound or video clips	Text Images Audio or video already formatted	Producer Writer Graphic designer Software developer
A CD-ROM with animated interactive content	Text Images Audio Animation	Producer Writer Graphic designer Animator Software developer
An interactive, animated Web presentation	Text Images Audio Animation	Producer Writer Graphic designer Animator Web developer

Project Type	Media Used	Talent Needed
A CD-ROM with animated interactive content and audio and video	Text Images Audio Video Animation	Producer Writer Graphic designer Animator Audio/video producer Software developer
A Web-based interactive game with audio and video	Text Images Audio Video Animation	Producer Writer Graphic designer Animator Audio/video producer Web developer
TV/Internet convergence*	Text Images Audio Video	Producer Writer Graphic designer Audio/video producer Web developer Telecommunications expert

*Convergence means the combination of two things. In this case it is the combination of the television industry and the Web industry.

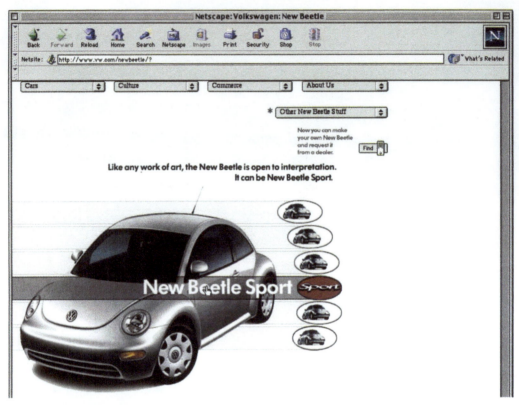

Netscape: Volkswagen: New Beetle

Volkswagen's Web site has advanced interactivity that enables users to inspect cars almost as though they were looking at the vehicles in person.

music or video, they are inspired to purchase items they may not have in the past. Multimedia sampling helps CDNOW increase its total profits.

Volkswagen

The auto retailer Volkswagen uses highly complex animations to highlight its range of cars on its company Web site. Users can interact with the site to navigate sections and look at 3-D models of VW vehicles. These 3-D models turn and zoom in and out with the click of a mouse. Interactivity allows Web site users to gain access to information about Volkswagen products while creating an engaging experience for customers. Volkswagon's multimedia Web site creates a positive impression of Volkswagen as a company.

Nike

With widespread use of the Internet increasing every day, more companies use the Web to create interactive experiences to promote a product, service, or brand. Nike, the popular footwear and sportswear company, employed Zendo Studios to create Mindsprint—an interactive game that doubles as an effective Web site marketing tool. Mindsprint uses entertaining, interactive visuals to give users information about Nike's line of Presto footwear. Users have fun while learning about Nike's gear, and the interactivity of the Web site creates a positive, memorable impression of Nike as a brand.

MULTIMEDIA AND E-COMMERCE PROMOTION

Some e-tailers balked at customer complaints about downloading fancy multimedia animations. Other click-and-mortar stores (established retailers with a

Kiosks are growing in popularity because they enable users to access information and order products any time of the day or night.

physical store as well as an online presence) got busy. Retailers began hiring professionals in the multimedia industry to create programs to run on in-store kiosks (public computer stations placed inside a retail store where customers can search the company's Web site or gather additional information about goods and services). This experiment has been a satisfying one in terms of customer service.

Kiosks

If you have ever been to a Borders bookstore or some of the flagship Gap stores, you may have seen or used a computer kiosk. A popular multimedia advancement for retailers, kiosks are predicted to be the wave of the future, popping up all over the place throughout the next decade. What can you do with kiosks and why are they important multimedia tools? The answer is simple: increased customer satisfaction. Customers can access important information at a kiosk, such as detailed service agreements and product information, contracts, warranties, and more. Some customers even shop at computer kiosks within the actual store, like the young people at Gap's new, relaxed Web Lounge. According to Rebecca Weill, a Gap company spokeswomen, the Web lounges are "always crowded."

Retailers noticed the importance of kiosks after research showed the level of interaction between online and offline sales. According to Activmedia Inc., an Internet research firm, 54 percent of click-and-mortar stores report "a substantial interaction between online and offline sales." This is one of the reasons kiosks are projected to be so successful.

Retailers are responding. Kiosks may be found today in many retail chain stores, including Sears,

Gap, Compaq Computer, and Borders bookstores. Some kiosks are even becoming popular in major supermarket chains! Supermarket kiosks can be utilized to access recipes and to place food orders in other departments, such as the deli or bakery, saving customers valuable time.

COMPANIES IN THE MULTIMEDIA BUSINESS

Many companies create multimedia products and/or projects, including software development firms, entertainment companies, educational software companies, and Web development companies of all sizes. The following are several examples of companies that are exploring multimedia resources.

Macromedia

Macromedia is the premier developer of multimedia software products—the software that other people use to create multimedia experiences on Web sites or for products such as CD-ROMs. Macromedia is best known for creating Flash—a development tool for creating interactive animated content. Macromedia also distributes the popular Flash Player, a browser plug-in that enables users to view animated content in the Flash format. Currently, 96.4 percent of computers have the Flash plug-in installed, making it the standard software for viewing animated content. Macromedia also makes other software products, such as Macromedia Director and Macromedia FreeHand, to create complex animations.

Macromedia is also known for creating shockwave.com—one of the first Web sites purely devoted to online interactive gaming. This Web site is a showcase of multimedia games, including some created by famous cartoonists.

Disney

Disney maintains a variety of Web sites, from sites devoted to its upcoming movies, which showcase both audio and video clips, to sites about its theme parks, which utilize animation. Disney also has its company's presence on the Internet, with sites about its history, including animations featuring its popular cartoon characters. Disney creates CD-ROMs on various educational subjects that include audio and video components as well as interactivity. Disney is famous for having a job position called an Imagineer, which covers a broad range of talents but includes illustration, animation, and audio and video engineering.

Multimedia Basics

When creating multimedia projects, creative and technical people work together to take static text and merge it with graphics, video, audio, and animation to develop exciting applications for use in CD-ROMs or on the Internet.

CONTENT

The content that can be used to create a multimedia project includes four types: text, graphics, audio, and video.

Text

Text can be created specifically for a multimedia project or it can be taken from an existing source, such as a brochure, book, magazine, or other document. Text written for multimedia projects must be short in length. Research has shown that online users have less patience

Graphics such as these at Yahoo! allow Web users to easily and quickly identify and find the services they seek.

when reading online. When text competes with other elements on the Web page for the users' attention, they can become easily distracted. Large blocks of text are uncommon on Web sites that use multimedia.

Graphics

Multimedia designers use a variety of graphics, including photographs, illustrations, and digital images. These images, when digitized, contain thousands of tiny squares, or pixels, that make up the picture on a computer screen.

21

Photographs must be scanned into the computer using a scanner and a software program such as Adobe Photoshop, or the photograph must already be in a digital format. In either case, photographs tend to be very detailed, especially color photographs. Color photos contain more digital information than do black-and-white images. Because it would take a very long time to download a colorful image that contains so much data, every effort must be made by the designer to diminish this information. Graphic designers do this by decreasing the number of colors used and by lowering the image's resolution, that is, the number of pixels the image contains. By applying both of these downgrades, the actual graphic, or the file that contains its binary information, becomes much smaller in size. Smaller files download quickly. If the photograph contained all of its original information, it could take a much longer time to download, which could result in a potential user moving on to another Web site.

Illustrations, like photographs, are also scanned into computers but are typically created in software programs such as Adobe Illustrator or FreeHand. Illustrations are commonly used as icons, logos, or diagrams that demonstrate how something works. Also, digital images are created nearly entirely with software programs (known as imaging software) such as Photoshop. Illustration or photography may be a part of the original image, but it is created online instead of shot with a camera or drawn by an artist and scanned into a computer.

All digital images must be compressed (made as small as possible in terms of the amount of disk space used) and put into a file format. These formats can be "read" and used either in CD-ROM or in Web production. File formats include bitmaps, GIFs, and JPEGs.

After images are scanned or created, they may be altered by the designer through the use of software filters. Graphics software filters are used as tools in much the same way that a painter uses a brush or a photographer uses a camera lens. Images may be retouched, distorted, multiplied, and completely transformed using any number of basic tools.

Audio

Before any audio can be added to a Web site, it must be converted to, or originally produced in, digital formats that are a series of ones and zeros. This is called binary code. Digital formats are the only formats that computers can read and understand. Once audio is in digital (numerical) format, it needs to be compressed and put into a format that can be used in production. File formats include AU, AIFF, WAVE, and MPEG. Audio content must be handled carefully because the files tend to be large. Like computer graphics, audio files can take a long time to download. This extensive downloading time may be frustrating to users on lower bandwidths. (Bandwidth refers to the speed of a user's connection to the Internet.) The quality of the sound can also be greatly affected by different bandwidth connections. Many multimedia efforts take advantage of streaming technologies that load the audio as it is being heard. Streaming audio does not have to be downloaded completely before the entire file is heard. In other words, you could hear a song at the same time your computer is reading its information.

Video

Like audio, video must be in a digital format, so it has to be either created digitally or converted to digital. Video in digital format is a series of still images called frames. Frames are easy to imagine if you have ever seen a cartoon flipbook or a piece of actual 16 mm or 35 mm film. Think of frames as separate installments of the digital video, shown so quickly that it is easy to interpret the images as moving, or streaming. Video is especially in need of streaming, otherwise it can take a very long time to download. Video that is streaming improperly often looks choppy and disrupted.

POPULAR MULTIMEDIA DEVELOPMENT PROGRAMS

There are many programs on the market for designers and developers to create multimedia projects. New multimedia software is entering the market every day. The following are a few of the most widely used programs.

Flash

Flash is a popular program that allows a designer or an animator to create animations using both images and text. The designer or animator can also add sound and create "triggers" within the animation that correspond to a user's activity. Triggers are buttons or hotspots on which users can click their mouse for more information, or access a new screen. Flash can be used for simple animated navigation, or for complex presentations that require both moving text and images. Sound can be added to an application using Flash so that the animations contain streaming audio that is in sync (matched in time) with the animated graphics. Whenever you are moving through the levels of your favorite video game, for instance, if the animated characters are also speaking or singing with moving mouths, then the sound and the animation are in sync with each other.

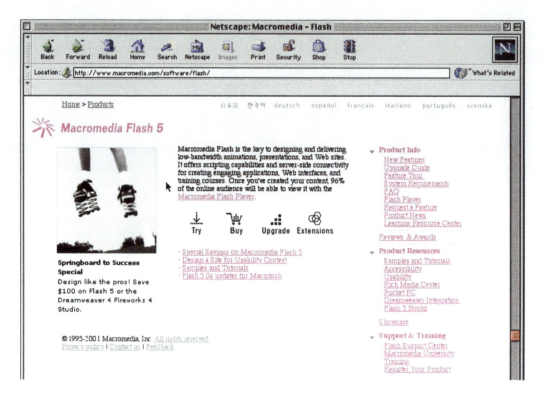

Web designers use Macromedia Flash to design animations, presentations, and Web sites. Once designers have created their content, some 96 percent of the online audience are able to view it with the free Flash Player.

Director

The software program called Director is more advanced than Flash. Normally, Director is used for creating animated, interactive experiences that require a high degree of programming for user activities, such as with video games and CD-ROMs. Animators who use Director often use a combination of text, images, and audio to create the overall program. Many triggers are programmed into the product to help create applications for increased user interaction. Any interactive experience with a 3-D quality was probably created by using Director software.

Adobe Photoshop

Adobe Photoshop is the standard program used by designers to alter photographs and create graphics for use on Web pages. Designers will often create entire Web pages using Photoshop. This popular software has become a computer graphics industry standard and offers designers a number of different tools to create varied image effects. These effects often include producing shadows, patterns, and text. Photoshop allows designers to shrink, flip, or enlarge images, add texture, change colors, blur edges, create distortions, or make any number of other changes. The options that designers have are nearly limitless when it comes to creating graphics.

Adobe Illustrator and Macromedia Freehand

Adobe Illustrator is often used to create textual images. These images are then opened with Photoshop and are added to another image. This program is also used to create illustrations. Freehand is a software program commonly used for creating 3-D illustrations.

POPULAR VIEWING PROGRAMS

Oftentimes, a user must have a plug-in for his or her browser that allows the browser to display different formats of multimedia information. Here are a few of the most commonly used plug-ins.

RealPlayer

Nearly every recent computer model comes with the RealPlayer plug-in already installed. This multimedia plug-in allows both audio and video content to be displayed either in a "player" (a separate program that appears as a new window on your computer screen) or directly within the Web page. The RealPlayer software displays audio and video formats created specifically for it.

Windows Media Player

Like the RealPlayer, the Windows Media Player is already installed on many computers. This multi-media plug-in also allows users to hear and view audio and video components. Like the RealPlayer, audio and video content is displayed either in a player or embedded into a Web page. This player displays a variety of audio and video formats.

Flash Player

The Flash plug-in allows users to view animated content in the Flash format. According to Macromedia, 96.4 percent of computers have the Flash Player plug-in installed, allowing more than 289 million computer users to view Flash content. This player works with the browser to display content within the browser window or Web page.

Shockwave Player

This multimedia plug-in allows users to view content created in Director using their Web browsers. Although this program is not as popular as the Flash Player, its popularity is steadily rising as more multimedia content is published directly on the Web.

Anatomy of a Multimedia Project

E very multimedia project is different. Each one combines familiar elements in a combined and creative way. Much of the world of multimedia takes preexisting text and merges it with moving imagery, photographs, video, film, and music. Almost any separate and artistic element can be combined to form one single multimedia message.

This chapter illustrates two examples that demonstrate what it takes to get a multimedia project completed. Although each one is very different, each will go through separate stages of planning, design, production, and testing.

ANIMATED PRESENTATIONS

Company X employed the firm of Image Nation to create an animated presentation of a new product line of running shoes. The company that produced the

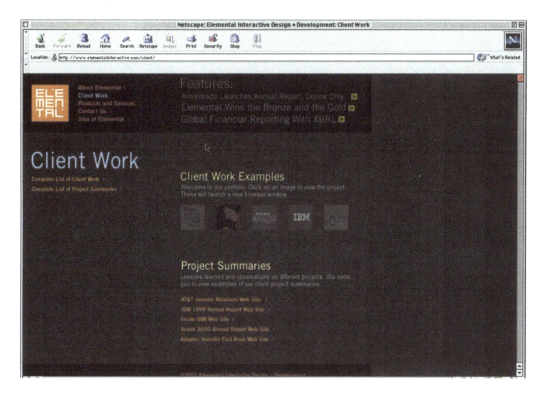

Multimedia projects require planning, design, production, and testing.

footwear wanted the presentation to highlight why the running shoes that they had created were better than their competitors' gear. After the project was completed, the animated short was going to be added to the company's existing Web site.

Planning

Before any animation could occur, the project had to be planned. A project schedule had to be set that allowed time for each stage of the design to be completed. Image Nation assigned a project manager, or producer, to the project. The producer worked with the company to determine the requirements of the project. The producer had to ask questions like, who was the intended audience? From where would the content come? When did the project need to be finished? What type of presentation did the company want? Would that same presentation be an effective one for an Internet audience? Once those basic answers were established, the actual work could begin. Image Nation would have four weeks to complete the project.

The company wanted an animated presentation that highlighted important points, such as which characteristics set the new running shoes apart from others produced by competitors. To do this, Image Nation needed additional information. They asked questions about the construction of the footwear and about the testing that the company had done on its gear. What they discovered was that the sport shoes had elaborate support that helped to decrease the impact that athletes felt while running. The extra support resulted from a newer, sturdier, and more lightweight plastic. In trial testing and research, the company found that an athlete's knees and ankles absorbed far less impact while he or she was wearing the newly designed and supportive footwear.

With this information, the project leader determined the necessary team members—a project leader who would also act as the content developer, a designer/animator, and a Web developer. Next, the producer assigned each team member to a schedule and began collecting the necessary content.

Design

Once the content was collected, the project manager/content developer created a detailed outline of the content to be included in the animated presentation. The presentation would be displayed in its own window and the user would click from one screen to the next. Using the company's research, the project manager created an outline of important points. Next, she gave each point in the outline a short title. These titles would be displayed at the top of each screen created in the animation. Then, the project manager/content developer determined whether a graphic or text would be displayed for each point. The text was written, and charts, tables, and graphics were selected for each point.

After the content outline was completed, it was handed off to the designer/animator. He designed the overall look and feel of the presentation, selecting the colors and fonts to be used, as well as the size of the presentation. Using the software program Flash, he took the text and charts and created a series of screens. Each screen displayed the title and some animation—either text fading in or charts that were animated as the user viewed them. Once each screen was produced, the designer/animator assembled them together in one digital file.

Production

After the designer completed the Flash animation, the files were handed off to the Web developer who then took it and embedded (put it into) an HTML (hypertext markup language) file. Finally, the Web developer created another Web page that would launch (open) a new browser window containing the HTML file together with the Flash file.

Testing

Once the presentation was completed, the project manager tested the application on a variety of browsers and platforms to ensure that it worked correctly. Any problems (bugs) were then fixed and the application was retested. Once the application was free of error, the files (both the Flash and HTML) were given to Image Nation to install on their own servers and launched. Many times, industry insiders call this a time when the Web site "goes live."

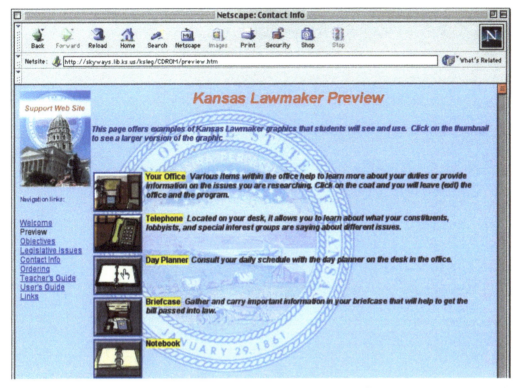

The development of the Kansas Lawmaker CD-ROM for the Kansas Board of Education required extensive planning and design.

INTERACTIVE CD-ROMS

The Kansas Board of Education employed a CD-ROM developer to create Kansas Lawmaker, an interactive CD-ROM to teach sixth- through ninth-graders about the lawmaking process. This complex project included using audio and video as well as using interactivity. It was designed based upon students exploring in a free-form manner rather than going through the content in a more structured style, such as an online book.

Planning

Before starting a project of this complexity, significant planning needed to be done. First, the project manager met with the board of education to determine what information needed to be included in the project. He created a list of objectives, or the goals that the client wished to achieve with the project. These objectives included why the project was undertaken, who the intended audience was, how the software would be viewed, and whether or not other materials would need to be shown with it. Using this information, a project manager was able to create a "headword" list, or a list of every topic that would become a part of the CD-ROM.

After the initial objectives were decided, more detailed planning was necessary. At this stage, the project manager worked with the client to determine what content should be included in the project. Content is normally determined by specific details. For example, in order to teach students how a bill becomes a law, it would be necessary to include content on the steps involved in the lawmaking process, and who and what is involved. After determining what content to include, the treatment of the content was specified. Treatment explains how each piece of content—audio, video, images, and text—will be presented. For example, to present the content on how a bill becomes a law, a short video or an animated illustration could be created. Every decision regarding how content is treated would be determined at this time.

The next step was for the project manager, while working closely with an instructional designer, to create a detailed outline of the project's content. This outline explained how each piece of content would be treated, and how it all worked together. The outline also determined which style of navigation would be used. Other decisions were made at this time also, such as which specific types of media would be used, which presentation styles (games, quizzes, videos) would be designed, and what the nature of the interactivity (buttons, links, or random events) would be. To answer these questions, the project manager created a navigation blueprint to explain how the user could navigate through the software.

Finally, using the detailed content outline, the project manager determined the team players needed to produce the application. He created a schedule and a budget for the project. The team players chosen included a project manager, an instructional designer, a software developer, a graphic designer, two graphic design interns, and some freelance support from an audio/video production team.

Design

Working from the content outline, the team assembled an application design document. This creation acted as a proposal. To produce the content, subject matter experts were employed. These experts needed to be involved in creating the application design document, as well as the subject matter that determined how the content would flow. This document, or flowchart, also provided the details about how each component would be built, about which software programs would be used, and how the size of the files affected the software's efficiency. The flowchart also demonstrated how the software would interact with the viewer.

Next, the team created detailed storyboards (boxed illustrations that show each individual screen, or component of a larger application, and how they relate to each other). Multimedia teams also call these detailed illustrations scamps, or pencil layouts, that show the position of the text and images on every screen. The scamps, or storyboards, are visual representations of the content. They are based on specific content outlines for each individual piece, and decisions about how pieces will work together. Using these layouts, individual team members designed their own piece of the project assigned to them.

Designers often review scamps, or storyboards, illustrating the individual frames of multimedia content.

Development

First, the designer created an overall look and feel for the software. Next, the software developer took the design and created a prototype, or a working demonstration. The prototype showed how the finished product would look and how the navigation worked. The prototype also established how the interactivity would work.

At this point in the development phase, the project manager created a more detailed schedule, including information on each component's progress.

Content was created by the appropriate team members, who recorded audio, shot video, wrote text, and took photographs. All of this content was edited, compressed, and delivered in the proper format to both the project designer and developer. Finally, the designer and the developer worked together to create the software application.

Testing

A project of this complexity goes through three stages of testing—alpha, beta, and omega. Alpha testing is the first stage, and it occurs when the application is nearly completed—all functionality is in place, which means that the software is working, but some content may be missing. This allows the developers additional time to repair any major problems that may arise. Project managers are alerted to bugs in the software when the test program stops working. Many times, programmers must search through hundreds of lines of programming to find the bugs, or the source code errors that may have caused the crash.

Beta testing is done when all content is fully integrated into the application. Development should be completed by this stage. Finally, omega testing is done once all bugs identified in the beta stage have been eliminated. Once omega testing is completed, the project is ready to be shipped.

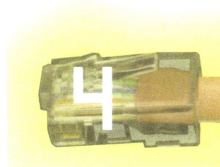

Careers in Multimedia

As you can see, many exciting opportunities exist within the field of multimedia. Any successful project needs a variety of people to participate and contribute to its development. Because multimedia environments can vary drastically, some of the roles people play will often be combined. For example, one person may fulfill the role of graphic designer and animator. Also, a person who is an expert at programming may also act as a content writer. Almost any combination is possible, but some of the basic multimedia positions are explained in this chapter.

GRAPHIC DESIGNER

This person is responsible for the overall look and feel of the multimedia piece. A graphic designer makes decisions regarding the selection of colors and fonts, determines the navigation style used, and creates all the graphics that are necessary for the project. This person typically uses Photoshop, Illustrator, and FreeHand to create images.

Although he or she is primarily responsible for the creative aspects of the project, a graphic designer must understand the technology that will be used to display his or her designs. For instance, a graphic designer must understand the rules for Web designing, such as file-size limitations and the variety of ways in which Web browsers display content. In most cases, the multimedia industry attracts highly talented visual artists who combine a variety of traditional talents, such as painting, drawing, and illustrating, with more technical computer skills.

ANIMATOR

Much like a graphic designer, an animator bridges the gap between the creative and the technical. On one hand, animators create a visual experience. On the other hand, they use complex software to manipulate pieces of content to move and to act. This process is much like how a developer might create a software application. The animator works closely with the

Graphic designers bring together the important elements of multimedia content—text, graphics, and animation.

graphic designer and takes content, such as text and imagery, and uses it to create animated content.

Animation can be applied to a variety of software. The Internet uses animated navigation that combines several images to create the appearance of movement. Gaming software uses animation with movement that interacts with the users' activity. The animator may also need to use 3-D modeling. Three-dimensional modeling is often used in the creation of computer games side by side with complex software applications. These applications specify behaviors (what the application does) for user activity such as clicking or moving through an area with the mouse. Animators typically use tools such as Flash, Director, and FreeHand to create animations.

WEB OR SOFTWARE DEVELOPERS

Developers use programming languages to create Web or software applications that display animation, video, and image content and that play audio content. The developer understands how to use different file formats and how to make those formats work together. He or she works closely with the designers, animators, and audio/video producers to take raw files and assemble them together, creating a multimedia result. Developers may use Flash, Director, or any number of programming languages, including HTML, JavaScript, VBScript, Java, and C++.

AUDIO/VIDEO PRODUCERS

People who produce audio and video typically use advanced computer-based programs and hardware that allow them to convert existing audio or video files into digital formats. More commonly, however, audio and video are created in digital formats using digital recorders and digital cameras.

Audio producers may manipulate sound and music a great deal—enhancing sounds or removing sounds altogether, such as background noise. Video producers may edit video to add, remove, or change its content. Once the audio or video content is edited, it is compressed (made as small as possible) and given to the developer or animator, who will put the condensed files into the larger application or make them available from another application, such as a Web page.

CONTENT EDITOR/DEVELOPER

Content editors/developers may write content themselves or may repurpose content that has been created already for something else. This person may determine whether content is needed for the entire application or may write or edit pieces outlined by the producer of the project. Either way, a content editor/developer needs to have a thorough understanding of how people read online—they read in short spurts of time and absorb small amounts of information. He or she also needs to understand where and how the created text will be used. Text created for animation may be very different from text created for a static page. Finally, he or she needs to understand the end user, so that the final copy created will appeal to the intended audience.

PRODUCER/PROJECT MANAGER

Producers, also called project managers, organize, plan, and manage the project and its team members throughout the entire length of the project's development. Producers need to have a thorough understanding of the project's scope, its audience, and the technology used to create it. Having a complete understanding of the elements of a multimedia project is necessary to successfully communicate its objectives, make appropriate scheduling decisions, and offer guidance to each team member. The producer is responsible for making sure the project is created on time and that it is completed within the specified budget.

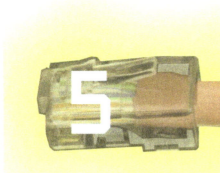

Getting Started

T he world of multimedia can be a fun, exciting place, but it can also be a lot of hard work. Before considering a career in the field of multimedia, you should know more about the skills and education needed. You should also know the amount of current growth potential in the industry.

LIFESTYLE

Multimedia companies come in all shapes and sizes—from the interactive division of a large firm such as Disney to small Web or software development companies such as Electronic Arts. In either case, multimedia companies tend to exist in major metropolitan areas and to employ young, creative, enthusiastic individuals. Because multimedia is a fast-paced industry, deadlines rule. Employees may be required to work long hours to get a project done. Fortunately, most people enjoy careers in the field of multimedia and have similar interests, so despite, or perhaps because of, the long hours, the feeling of comradery is strong. To counterbalance the long hours and hectic deadlines, multimedia companies tend to offer flexibility in other ways. It is typical to have flexible work hours, a casual environment (jeans and T-shirts), free beverages, frequent social gatherings, and, sometimes, the ability to bring your pet to work.

SKILLS NEEDED

Specific skills will depend on what you want to do. For instance, to be an effective designer you will need to learn about basic design techniques, such as effective use of color, typography (the study of fonts and type), composition (how items are arranged on a page), and layout. Animators and video/audio producers will need training in specific software programs. Developers need training in several programming languages and software programs.

To be successful, designers need to know about fonts and type, how items are best arranged on a page, and how to use color.

Beyond skills specific to your role, multimedia projects are very team oriented—you will need to be able to get along and work well with a variety of people. This requires the ability to communicate clearly, to work toward a common goal, and to be responsible for your part in the larger picture. You should also be very flexible and willing to do things that may not be a part of the typical job description in your field. Helping others and sharing responsibility makes an effective multimedia team.

Finally, a genuine interest in learning about technology and creating exciting, interactive projects goes a long way. Everyone wants to work on interesting projects; a willingness to dig in and learn about a variety of multimedia elements (design, animation, and technology) will make you very successful in the industry.

EDUCATION

There are as many ways into the multimedia industry as there are projects. Although the majority of people do have a college education, many do not hold degrees that relate to what they do in their jobs. Because parts of the industry are so new, many people simply entered the industry from the beginning. Graphic designers in print media sometimes made the switch to the Web, computer programmers occasionally crossed over into multimedia programming, and so on. Employers do prefer a college degree, but enthusiastic, talented individuals without college degrees will find that a combination of training and persistence can land them a well-paying and highly creative job.

College

For those who do decide to go to college, new degree programs are created every day that are specific to the computer, Internet, and multimedia industries. Designers and animators may choose to go to an art school that offers programs specific to the industry. Those interested in Web or software development careers may choose an engineering school with a curriculum in Internet and multimedia programming. Producers and content developers may choose more generalized majors, such as journalism or business.

Training

For those who do not want to go to college, or for those who want to continue their adult education, many training options are available. Local community colleges with continuing-education programs have created specific certificates for classes in computer-related design and development. These include design, animation, Web development, writing, and project management courses. There are also many national small training institutions, such as the Computer Learning Center or New Horizons, which have similar programs.

Internships

Nothing beats experience. Multimedia companies often have internship programs for college or high-school students who are considering a career in the industry. Because there is so much work to be done, interns are a valuable part of any multimedia team. Many interns are paid a small stipend for what they do, but for those who are not paid, college credits may be available. To find an internship, check out a company's Web site or call its human resources department. Many larger companies, such as Dell Computers, IBM, Apple Computer, and others, offer formal internship programs. If the company doesn't have a formal program, they may still be interested in hiring an intern to help out.

IN CONCLUSION

As technology becomes more of a part of our lives, the use of interactive, engaging media will continue to grow. The people creating these projects are just at the beginning of an exciting adventure. Multimedia itself is still very much in its infancy. For those thinking of entering into a dynamic and creative computer career in positions in graphic design, animation, and Web site production, keep in mind that these positions are on the cutting edge of both technology and creativity.

Glossary

animation   Drawn motion files, either in 2-D or 3-D. On the Web, HTML's push-pull animation is very low-end. JAVA, VRML, animated GIFs, Flash, and Shockwave are best adapted for Web animation.

bandwidth   The "pipe" through which information must be pumped. The larger the amount of data that needs to be delivered, the larger the pipe needs to be. This is currently the biggest limitation to delivering large amounts of digital video in multimedia. Optical fiber provides one of the largest pipes available.

bitmap   A computer graphic image composed of dots of color that correspond directly to data bits stored in memory.

browser   A device that allows users to peruse the contents of a hypermedia program, generally by providing some kind of overview, such as a contents list, from which the user may choose items of interest.

CD-ROM (compact disc read-only memory)
A circular disk that can hold around 650 megabytes of data. Information on a CD-ROM is read-only.

compression (file)   The process that reduces a file's size, often called zipping or archiving. The resulting compressed file can be from a single, large file, or can contain several files that have been squeezed together. The many-to-one compression makes file group identification, copying, and transporting faster and easier.

compression (video)   The process that reduces the number of bytes required to store/transmit digital video. Typical schemes involve comparing frames and coding-out, or eliminating, interframe and intraframe redundancies. The compression may be done by software, hardware, or a combination of the two. On playback, the data is decompressed.

digital audio   Sounds stored in a digital format.

digitized   To translate analog data into digital data so that it can be used and manipulated by the computer.

font   A style of type such as BauerBodoni, Century Schoolbook Bold, or Eurostile.

frame   A single picture in a computerized movie or digital video.

GIF (graphics interchange format) Compressed file format for graphics requiring a specific decoder to view.

hard disk   Permanent storage used to keep digitized information for future retrieval and use. Multimedia requires huge amounts of storage during both the development and application stages. Many multimedia products require storage on a CD-ROM.

hardware   The equipment needed to make and run multimedia programs. Hardware can include a computer, storage device, scanner, audio digitizer, and video frame-grabber.

hyperlink   In hypermedia, the programmed links between related items of information.

hypermedia   Interactive programs in which information is stored in a number of different media and cross-linked so that it can be retrieved and presented in a variety of ways. Hypermedia involves the presentation of information in media that most effectively communicates its content, and provides the user with the means to sequence information in ways that are most appropriate to a given task.

hypertext   A subset of hypermedia software with text documents that enable the user to read texts linked in a variety of linear and nonlinear ways, and create new links between words or passages of text.

HTML (hypertext markup language)   The programming language used to create simple Web pages.

icon   The pictorial representation of an object, a computer program, a feature, or a function within a hypermedia program.

interaction   The process of control and feedback between a user and the hypermedia system.

JPEG A graphic file format that can be viewed on Macintosh and PC.

links A feature of hypermedia programs that links associated items of information in different parts of a program.

MPEG A movie file format that can be viewed on Macintosh and PC.

multimedia Generic term for "multimedia computing" or "interactive multimedia." It is the combination of a wide variety of media.

navigation The process of finding one's way around the contents of a hypermedia program.

real-time Computer processing that takes place instantaneously.

scanner A piece of hardware for digitizing images. Scanners come in several versions, from grayscale to color, and are capable of scanning a variety of bit depths.

software Information such as computer programs, data, and hypermedia programs stored in digital form. Software controls hardware to make the computer perform certain functions.

TIFF A graphic file format that can be viewed on Macintosh and PC.

virtual reality (VR) The simulation of reality through real-time, 3-D animation, position tracking, and audio/video techniques. By immersing the user within a simulated computer-generated, simulated environment, VR systems introduce an entirely new way of interacting with multimedia information.

window Screen area that contains part or all of a computer program, such as a text window.

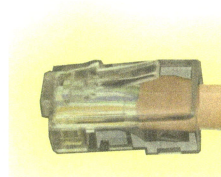

For More Information

IN THE UNITED STATES

Association of Internet Professionals (AIP)
The Empire State Building
350 Fifth Avenue, Suite 3018
New York, NY 10118
(877) AIP-0800 (247-0800)
Web site: http://www.association.org

Internet Alliance
1111 19th Street NW, Suite 1180
Washington, DC 20036-3637
(202) 955-8091
Web site: http://www.internetalliance.org

Web Design and Developers Association
8515 Brower
Houston, TX 77017

(435) 518-9784
Web site: http://www.wdda.org

IN CANADA

**Canadian Association of Internet
        Professionals**
P.O. Box 60015
RPO Glen Abbey
Oakville, ON L6M 3H2
Web site: http://www.caipnet.ca

WEB SITES

Association for Applied Interactive Multimedia
http://www.aaim.org

**Interactive Multimedia Arts & Technologies
        Assocation**
http://www.imat.ca

MultiMediator—Canada's Multimedia Guide
http://www.multimediator.com

NewMedia
http://www.newmedia.com

For Further Reading

Elliot, Joe and Time Worsley, eds. *Multimedia: The Complete Guide to CD-ROMs, the Internet, the World Wide Web, Virtual Reality, 3-D. Games, and the Information Superhighway.* New York: DK Publishing, 1996.

Graham, Lisa. *The Principals of Interactive Design.* Albany, NY: Delmar Publishers, 1999.

Johnson, Nels. *Web Developer's Guide to Multimedia and Video.* Scottsdale, AZ: Coriolis Book Group, 1996.

Peck, Dave. *Multimedia: A Hands-On Introduction.* Albany, NY: Delmar Publishers, 1997.

Peck, Dave. *Pocket Guide to Multimedia.* Albany, NY: Delmar Publishers, 1999.

Street, Rita. *Computer Animation: A Whole New World.* Gloucester, MA: Rockport Publishers, Inc., 1998.

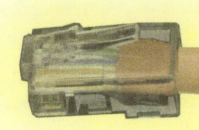

Index

A

Adobe Illustrator, 22, 27, 42
Adobe Photoshop, 22, 23, 27, 42
Ambron, Sue Ann, 4
animated presentations, 30
animation, 8, 19, 20, 25, 34, 46
animators, 5, 25, 33, 41–42, 44
  skills needed, 48
Apple Computer, 4, 52
application design document, 38
audio, 8, 10, 20, 23–24, 36,
  40, 45
audio engineers, 19
audio/video producers, 44–45
  skills needed, 48

B

bitmaps, 23
Borders bookstore, 17
business-to-business (B2B), 11
business-to-consumer (B2C), 11

C

CDNOW, 11
CD-ROMs, 4, 5, 8, 18, 26, 35,
  36, 38, 39
click-and-mortar stores, 15–16
college, 51
content developer, 33, 45–46
  skills needed, 48
Computer Learning Center, 51
content writer, 41

D

Dell Computers, 52
Director, 10, 19, 26–27, 29, 44
Disney, 19, 47

E

Electronic Arts, 47
e-tailers, 5, 6, 11, 15

F

film, 30

Flash, 10, 18–19, 25, 33, 34, 44
Flash Player, 29
flowchart, 38
FreeHand, 19, 22, 27, 42, 44

G

Gap stores, 17
    Web lounge, 17
GIFs, 23
graphic designers, 5, 21, 27,
        33, 37, 41–44, 48
    skills needed, 48
graphics, 4, 8, 20–23

H

"headword" list, 36
HTML, 34, 44

I

IBM, 52
Image Nation, 31, 32
instructional designer, 37
interactivity, 4–5, 8, 19
internships, 52
Internet, 4, 5, 32

J

JavaScript, 44
JPEGs, 23

M

Macromedia, 18–19
Mindsprint, 15
music, 30

N

New Horizons, 51
Nike, 15

P

pixels, 21
producer, 32, 46
project managers, 32, 33, 36,
        37, 40, 46

R

RealPlayer, 28
rich media, 5, 8, 10

S

shockwave.com, 19
Shockwave Player, 29
skills, 48–49
software developers, 5, 37, 44
storyboards, 38

T

testing, 40
text, 4, 8, 20, 30, 36, 40, 43
training, 51

V

VBScript, 44
video, 4, 8, 10, 14, 20, 24, 30,
        36, 40, 45
Volkswagen, 14–15

W

Web developers, 33, 34, 44
Web sites, 6, 8, 10, 16, 19, 31, 34

ABOUT THE AUTHOR

Carla Romain Cowan lives in Berkley, California, and is the cofounder of Symbiosis, Inc., an online media venture for organizations and individuals working for social change. Prior to Symbiosis, she worked as the director of online services for Experience, Inc. She has also worked has a project manager, Web developer, and writer for various agencies involved in the production of multimedia projects.

PHOTO CREDITS

P. 6 © www.gap.com; p. 9 © www.bn.com; p. 14 © www.vw.com; p. 16 © Bell Atlantic/AP/Worldwide; p. 21 © www.yahoo.com; p. 26 © www.macromedia.com; p. 31 © www.elementalinteractive.com; p. 35 © skyways.lib.ks.us/ksleg/CDROM/preview; p. 39 by Ira Fox; p. 43 © AP/Worldwide; p. 49 by Cindy Reiman.

SERIES DESIGN

Les Kanturek

www.ingramcontent.com/pod-product-compliance
Lightning Source LLC
Chambersburg PA
CBHW050937060326
40689CB00040B/612